Mary's Night

POEMS by

Angela Albano

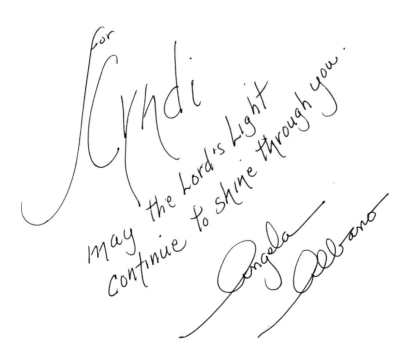

For Cyndi
may the Lord's Light
continue to shine through you.
Angela Albano

DEDICATION

For Mary, the courageous teenager, who said yes to the call of God to be the mother of Jesus the Christ.

For you, the reader, may you answer God's call on your life to a commitment beyond your circumstances and reap the extraordinary blessings He has for you.

CONTENTS

ILLUSTRATIONS

Mary and the Angel
The Annunciation, James Tissot (1836-1902)

Joseph and the Dream
The Vision of Saint Joseph, James Tissot (1836-1902)

The Star
The Appearance of the Star,
Giovanni Da Modena (c. 1409-1456)

Bethlehem Donkey
Donkey, Johann Georg Grimm (1846-1887)

The Crowded Inn
Saint Joseph Seeks a Lodging in Bethlehem,
James Tissot (1836-1902)

The Barn-Cave
The Birth of Our Lord Jesus Christ,
James Tissot (1836-1902)

My Birthday
All the City Was Gathered at His Door,
James Tissot (1836-1902)

The Manger
Geburt Christi, Federico Barocci (1535-1612)

The Perfect Lamb
The Adoration of the Shepherds,
James Tissot (1836-1902)

One of the Angels
Music-Making Angel, Melozzo da Forli (1438-1494)

Bethlehem
Bethlehem, Vasily Polenov (1844-1927)

The Earth
Landscape Composition: St. John in the Wilderness,
Thomas Cole (1801-1848)

The Shepherds
The Angel and the Shepherds,
James Tissot (1836-1902)

Mary's Night
Adoration of the Shepherds 1622,
Gerard van Honthorst (1590-1656)

PREFACE

In this telling of the Christmas story, we hear not only from the people in the narrative, but also from animals, objects, and places intimately connected with the birth of Jesus.

If the donkey could talk, what would he say about his seven-mile trek from Nazareth to Bethlehem? If an angel could give her perspective from heaven, what would her thoughts be? If the manger that cradled Baby Jesus could speak, how would it describe holding the Son of God within its form? The barn-cave, the star, the town, a lamb — each has their own Christmas story to tell.

Every Christmas for more than a decade, I have written a Christmas poem for friends and family and, frankly, any-one who would read it. As the season drew near each year, I reread the Biblical account of Jesus' birth in the Gospel of Luke before beginning to write. The resulting poems differ in style and length and who was speaking. I was delighted to record the words of Mary, Joseph, and Jesus as they came to me. And I was intrigued to discover the animals and inanimate objects sharing their own meaningful experiences through my words.

Thinking like the Manger, or the Star, or the Bethlehem Donkey increases the holiness of the event for me as they share their participation in the miracle of Jesus' birth. The donkey has a long trip, so he has a lot to tell.

"The Crowded Inn" and "The Perfect Lamb" were written this year, 2011. The Inn's musings about the innkeeper's kindness and his ultimate rallying call are an opportunity to absolve the innkeeper from the role of the ogre-of-no-room. I enjoy his unexpected transformation.

"Oh, Little Town of Bethlehem," the subject of the ancient carol, had definite significance in its day. Holy bread for offering in the temple was baked there. In fact, the name "Bethlehem" means "House of Bread." And the lambs for temple sacrifice for the sins of the Israelites were raised there. These lambs had to be perfectly white with no blemish or physical defect. The little lamb the shepherd lays by Baby Jesus' side in "The Perfect Lamb" was just such a lamb from Bethlehem. His story is all the more poignant knowing what his end would be.

"Mary's Night" created in me a tender bond with Mary because of her unquestioning trust in God and her courage to agree to be part of His miracle. I wonder if she had a sense of the social repercussions she would face? Reading about Mary in the original language of the Bible suggests strongly that Mary was quite young, perhaps thirteen. I was impressed anew by how she transformed from a teenage daughter of peasant parents to the mother of the King of Kings. Mary answered God's call and, to this day, people call her blessed just as she said they would.

It pleases me to have all my Christmas poems in book form. Over the years I've presented them to friends, family, co-workers, students in this country and abroad, neighbors, people in the supermarket and in my post office. You now possess some well-traveled poems! I hope they rest peacefully in your home and become part of your Christmas tradition of songs, stories and poems about Mary's wondrous night when she gave birth to Jesus, the Son of God.

Christmas Blessings,

Angela

ACKNOWLEDGMENTS

This book has come together because of the people in my life who believed in me, encouraged me, and walked alongside me during the process. I am deeply grateful for their help and for sharing so much of themselves with me. Poetry brought us closer to one another, as only poetry can do.

Helen Compton-Jensen, my loving friend from art college, was taken from this earth too soon to celebrate the publishing of my first book. Helen, a publisher and writer, read many of my poems and enthusiastically offered advice and love in equal amounts. Most of all, Helen was a faithful friend.

Jennifer Elmore, an accomplished poet and writer, became my poetry mentor when I asked her if she would take on that role. Jennifer has a gentle way of inviting me to sit a while with my ideas, go deeper within myself, and watch the unfolding of hidden expressions and images. Jennifer is a woman of grace.

Timothy Hodges, writing and editing expert, edits my writing with aplomb and sprinkles his comments with encouragement the way my grammar school teachers gave out gold stars. Tim instills confidence in others.

Jan Innes came into my life at just the right moment. My Christmas poems written over the years had built up to a crescendo. It was time to gather them together to tell the story of the birth of Jesus. As we chatted in our Club IV room one day, I discovered that Jan knew how to design a book and how to e-publish. Jan made my dream come true.

Elizabeth Perea, my marketing consultant and daughter, has consistently cheered me on over the years by her comments, editing, and suggestions. I have been blessed to have her travel alongside me in my writing journey. Liz has a brilliant mind and a tender heart.

Mary Lynne McLintock at MarketingWorksTexas.com offered ideas, editing, solutions, and lovely final touches. Mimi has an endearing way about her and a generous, giving spirit.

Mary's Night

MARY AND THE ANGEL

A dazzling light turns my head away
with half-closed eyes I strain to see
what in my room has suddenly appeared
in the midst of my morning prayer.

Adjusting to the light I dare
to raise my head, my eyes, and peer,
slowly lifting up my gaze
till standing o'er me I can see

something or someone I have never seen,
a being bright and beautiful and clear.
He gives his name as Gabriel,
a messenger of God is he.

To him I listen attentively,
hardly believing the words I hear.
The Son of God will come from me,
a peasant girl from Galilee.

Why would He choose me, Mary,
when He could select nobility,
to be the mother of God the King?
I'm just a girl, not yet fifteen.

Questioningly, I wonder how I can be
a mother before being married.
The angel Gabriel says assuredly;
the Holy Spirit will plant His seed.

A son, therefore, will be born to me.
His birth is meant to set all free.
Jehovah-Saves, His name will be;
Jesus, the sound to my ears is sweet.

Luke 1:30-32

But the angel said to her,
"Do not be afraid, Mary,
you have found favor with God.
You will be with child
and give birth to a son,
and you are to give him the name Jesus.
He will be great
and will be called the Son of the Most High."

Luke 1:34-35

"How will this be," Mary asked the angel,
"since I am a virgin?"
The angel answered,
"The Holy Spirit will come upon you,
and the power of the Most High will overshadow you.
So the holy one to be born
will be called the Son of God."

JOSEPH AND THE DREAM

I never heard Gabriel's words.

Doubt caused me to reject the message.

But in a dream, revealed to me…

were wondrous words direct from heaven.
An angel visited me as well
and thereby put my mind at ease.
My role in life would now increase…
adoptive father to the King of Kings.

To Mary, I ran and pledged my love,
believing now our roles would be
to parent the long-awaited Messiah…
Hardly imagining all that could mean.

Now the baby's coming has filled us with awe.
Tonight angels, like stars, cover the sky.
I hold our newborn Son in my arms…
A universe of love streams from His eyes.

Quietly, quietly, we ponder the moment;
the Creator of Life is placed in our trust.
How He must love us to leave His heaven…
become a little baby, and live among us.

Matthew 1:20-21

But after he had considered this,
an angel of the Lord
appeared to him in a dream
and said, "Joseph son of David,
do not be afraid to take Mary home as you wife,
because what is conceived in her
is of the Holy Spirit.
She will give birth to a son,
and you are to give him the name Jesus,
because he will save his people from their sins."

Matthew 1:24-25

When Joseph woke up,
he did as the angel had commanded him
and took Mary home as his wife.
But he had no union with her
until she had given birth to a son.

14

THE STAR

I spread my streaming light...
       stretching across the darkened night,
my brilliance captures the eyes of many.

Astrologers from afar...
       seekers of knowledge in the stars,
know the miraculous message that I carry.

Looking down on the earth beneath...
       a greater light than mine I see;
a holy brilliance shines brighter than my own.

With upturned faces shepherds squint...
          in awe and disbelief in my extent;
I now share the sky with angels everywhere.

Moving slowly as I travel...
          to the place where lies a marvel,
in a stable filled with animals at peace.

My streams of silver mingle...
          with His tiny rays so golden;
now my mission to announce Him is complete.

Angels sing their hallelujahs;
          shepherds kneel in adoration;
A mother cradles in her arms the Prince of Peace.

My wondrous journey now is over,
          and my nights of silver splendor...
in Bethlehem will never fade from memory.

Matthew 2:1-2

After Jesus was born in Bethlehem in Judea,
during the time of King Herod,
Magi from the east came to Jerusalem and asked,
"Where is the one who has been born king of the Jews?
We saw his star in the east
and have come to worship him."

Matthew 2:9-10

After they had heard the king,
they went on their way,
and the star they had seen in the east
went ahead of them
until it stopped over the place where the child was.
When they saw the star,
they were overjoyed.

BETHLEHEM DONKEY

Ahead I see the hills of Bethlehem;
an unusually bright star has lighted our path.

The woman keeps shifting in her seat on my back;
discomfort has settled in; it's been a long trip.

She looks up anticipating an end to the bumping
and tipping and swaying.

We wait together while her man knocks on one door
after another,
looking for a place to rest—

A place to finally lie down
and feel the ache of the journey drain away.

I, too, will rest, eat some grass or grain,
drink some water,
and see why we came.

A long while later, we've stopped at a cave,
behind an inn
where some animals stay.

With the help of her man, the woman dismounts;
I wait to see what they will do now.

Amazingly, the star has stopped overhead; it's easy
to see inside the cave.
The place looks clean; I smell fresh hay.

The man helps his wife to get comfortable
off to one side away from the entrance.

He kindly gives me some water and grain, sets me
next to a cow
and lights a lantern.

At last we all lie down for some long-needed rest;
the star still shines brightly over our heads.

My eyes are heavy; it's been a long trip;
I welcome the quiet and lower my head.

Sleep comes quickly; the ache starts to fade;
the woman also must feel the same.

What's that sound that I hear? Talking and singing
up in the sky
and right next to me a new baby's cry?

It's happened! He's come! The baby's arrived
and who are all those people who know how to fly?

I blink and I stare, wondering what's going on;
my long donkey ears are filled with their song.

Singing and chanting fill the night air,
and all I can do is wonder and stare.

I'm so glad I was chosen to carry the Babe.
I can see He is special by the look on His face.

I feel His love touch me; how His love fills this place.
The star shines even brighter turning night into day.

Now sheep are mingling with us in the cave;
they've come with some shepherds to visit the Babe.

They quietly kneel to adore and treat Him like God,
this Babe of the woman that I carried and brought.

My eyes wide-open take all of this in;
I'll never forget what has happened.

I may be parked facing many a wall,
but my eyes will be filled with scenes of great awe.

Of a night full of wonder, a night full of song
when I was present at the birth of our Lord.

Luke 2: 1-5

In those days Caesar Augustus
issued a decree
that a census should be taken
of the entire Roman world….
And everyone went to his own town to register.
So Joseph also went up
from the town of Nazareth in Galilee
to Judea, to Bethlehem the town of David,
because he belonged to the house
and the line of David.
He went there to register with Mary,
who was pledged to be married to him
and was expecting a child.

THE CROWDED INN

My guest room is full of travelers
lying on bed mats, side by side;
night has fallen

snores float above them
merging with smoke
and warmth
from the communal fire.

I have a spacious room
without privacy, of course,
but I cannot house
one person more.

In anxious low tones,
I hear a man plead,
"Please, let us stay, at least, for tonight.
My wife's ridden a donkey
over mountain ridges and valleys
for almost a week.
And soon, very soon her baby will come.

Blocking my doorway, the innkeeper says firmly
"There's no room.
Plus the law forbids she give birth in here."
He steps outside,
sees the young mother
desperate for sleep and a place to lie down.
His whisper is clear in the cool night air,
"But, wait, go out back where you'll find a stable.
That's all I can offer in
her circumstances."

Outside my windows, silver starlight is streaming;
the couple sees plainly
the path to the barn.

And in that peaceful abode
after a while, her baby is born.
No curious stares
saw the woman's travail
only a cow,
a donkey,
and the eyes of God.

Silence has been unknown to me
all the moments I've stood;
the stones of my walls
listen
reflect
each word, murmur
and sound.
And now hovering above my roof
in the brightened night
is singing
I've never ever heard before.

Shepherds are hurrying down the hills
out my back door
headed to where a huge star
shines over the stable
where the couple is resting.

Beside them the Babe, asleep in the manger.
Near him shepherds are kneeling,
hands over their hearts.

Suddenly, across the sky angels are singing,
"Glory to God.
Peace on earth this wondrous night.'
The innkeeper is rushing to check on
what's happening
as the words of the prophets
flood into his mind.

I hear his voice
bellow
to awaken the travelers
"Come, come! See for yourselves."
Repeating the words of an angel
he shouts
"Here in Bethlehem this night,
The Messiah is born."

Luke 2: 6-7

While they were there,
the time came for the baby to be born,
and she gave birth to her firstborn, a son.
She wrapped him in cloths
and placed him in a manger,
because there was no room for them in the inn.

THE BARN-CAVE

"Mysterious how things work out—
Who would have thought
or even imagined
that I,
a cave in the tiny village of Bethlehem,
would be chosen to hold
within the confines of my stone
the Cornerstone of Mankind.

I have existed for eons,
since the world began —not unlike the
Ever-existing Child
being born this night.

No longer a cave of darkness am I,
infused as I've been by the
Giver of Light
this incredible Child,
long-awaited Messiah…
Jesus the Christ."

A cave used as a barn
has become the Holy Family's
embracer.

A cold, dark hide-a-way
carved out of ancient rock
housing a donkey, a cow and her calf…

Not much of a home
for the birthing of the Son of Man…
the Son of God —

the Creator of the Cave, Himself.

Luke 2:12

This will be a sign to you:
You will find a baby wrapped in cloths
and lying in a manger.

MY BIRTHDAY

My birthday is here
    a time filled with cheer
a time to recall my mission.

I left heaven's home
    to live and to roam
in a world that needed forgiveness.

My early years
    with my mother, Mary,
were filled with love and laughter.

Joseph, my dad,
    he was so glad
to teach me to be a carpenter.

Our family life
    had its share of strife,
but I enjoyed my sisters and brothers.

We played like all kids
    and the things that we did
were much like those of others.

At thirty things changed
    my life rearranged
my mission became the main focus.

The teaching was fine,
    the healing and signs,
I enjoyed helping people in trouble.

The best part though
    was when I showed
how they could get to heaven.

Some listened, accepted,
    some left disappointed
others angered, and put me to death.

All that took place
    was planned by God's grace
to provide a way to unite us.

I'm waiting for you
    I'm saving your room
You'll love living with me in my house.

Matthew 11:4-5

Jesus replied, "Go back and report to John
what you hear and see:
The blind receive sight,
the lame walk,
those who have leprosy are cured,
the deaf hear,
the dead are raised,
and the good news is preached to the poor."

THE MANGER

I am the manger that cradles the
Bread of Life,
the Child

who will grow to be the
Light of the World.

I, a trough of nourishment, hold
The One
who has come to
nourish all of us

to give to each person
Living Water,
to actually be that living water,
so that they will
thirst no more.

I, a trough of aliment, hold the
Giver of Life
the Sustainer of Life.

How blessed am I to shelter
in the boards of my body,
the delicate body of
The Child
who one day will be laid once more on a board,
a cross beam of wood
and once
and for all
give all
that He can,

so that all
who believe
will live on
into eternity.

This Child,
this Babe,
this Little One, snuggled so peacefully
in me, a trough,
in me,
a manger,
made of
wood
and
nails

.

Luke 2: 16

So they hurried off
and found Mary and Joseph, and the baby,
who was lying in the manger.

THE PERFECT LAMB

I bounce along in the arms of my shepherd,
too young, too small to walk on my own.

I fell asleep as twilight drew the sun into her cloak,
but now a bright star has brought back the day.

My pastor strides down a hill where my mother grazes;
the shoots of grass here are tender and sweet.
His sandals sink deeper, crushing the grass
as he shuffles with speed increasing.

Keeping up with the star, we reach the foot of the hill;
from the crook of his arm, I lift my eyes and see

the star shining whiter than wool in the night,
a firelight flickering from a barn-cave beneath.

Leaning forward, I tilt my head and see inside
a mother, a father, and a baby, small like me.

My shepherd, without words, kneels to worship the Babe
gently placing me close to the Infant.

The eyes of the Babe look deep into mine
with knowing He smiles with compassion.

Born with perfect white fleece here in Bethlehem,
my purpose in life was predestined.

I touch my nose to His arm and nuzzle His face;
His little hand strokes the crown of my head.

No other touch, no other hand has felt like His;
I bleat sounds of contentment and sense—

On this star-bright night, in this holy place,
I'm not the only sacrificial lamb.

John 1:29

The next day John saw Jesus
coming toward him and said,
"Look, the Lamb of God,
who takes away the sin of the world!"

1Peter 1:18-20

For you know
that it was not with perishable things
such as silver or gold
that you were redeemed
from the empty way of life
handed down to you
from your forefathers,
but with the precious blood of Christ,
a lamb without blemish or defect.
He was chosen
before the creation of the world,
but was revealed in these last times
for your sake.

ONE OF THE ANGELS

I am one of hundreds of angels looking down
from above,
moving back and forth across the midnight sky.

We see the Christ embodied in a baby boy;
our Lord's no longer in heaven; He's gone for a while.

Unfathomable happenings are occurring below.
The earth will house our Beloved One for a time.

We'll miss Him and watch His life from afar.
Nothing like this has ever happened before.

We can't imagine how events will go.
This night is glorious; will it always be so?

Here in heaven He held such a high place.
Now He's a baby; we wonder what He will face.

We already miss Him; He's never been gone.
How ever without Him, will we get along?

We'll continually watch over all that He does,
and never, no never, leave Him alone.

Oh, Babe in the manger, do You feel cold?
We'll come close to warm You as we sing our song.

Glory and praises to our Baby the King.
How unusual to see You in a manger sleeping.

So tiny and helpless, where has your power gone?
What wondrous things will You do in this land?

We'll be watching and waiting, wanting your return.
How long will we wait? How long will we yearn?

Will You come back and be as You were before?
Or will You look different for having sojourned?

So many questions come to my mind.
I'm just an angel, no answers I find.

But I will trust the Father knows where You will be,
and why He has sent You on your earthly journey.

For now, I will join in singing Glory to God
and peace of mind and soul to all that He loves.

Goodnight, dear Child, dear Prince of Peace;
in my heart, sweet memories of You will I keep.

Luke 2:13-14

Suddenly a great company
of the heavenly host
appeared with the angel,
praising God and saying,
"Glory to God in the highest,
and on earth peace to men on
whom his favor rests."

BETHLEHEM

The King of Heaven
Has resided in the womb
Of a young woman
Over the past few months.

Now, this night, in me, the
Sleepy little town of Bethlehem,
He is appearing
As no other living creature
That has ever lived:

Messiah and man,
God and baby boy,
Creator and creature,
Son of God and Son of Mary.

I am the city of David,
A city of kings,
Yet today the King of Kings is born.

Bethlehem: House of Bread,
City of temple bread…
Now home to the Bread of Life.
Town of sacrificial lambs,
Now birthplace to the Lamb of God.

Sing the song of Bethlehem,
How blessed I am.
The starry night proclaims my fame,
And now a new light…
A Guiding Light has come
In the form of a tiny babe,
Born in a remote stable,
Illuminated by a brilliant star.

The world, this night, in me,
Bethlehem
Has been visited by God Himself.

Micah 5:2

"But you, Bethlehem Ephrathah,
though you are small
among the clans of Judah,
out of you will come for me
one who will be ruler over Israel,
whose origins are from of old,
from ancient times."

THE EARTH

I lift the arms of my trees
to embrace Him.
I warm the waters of my pools
to bathe Him.
I tune the choirs of my zephyrs

to sing to Him.
I awaken the mountains
to protect Him.
I coax the golden sun streams
to nestle in His hair.

I…the earth my God created…
announce
from the depths of my canyons
to the height of my clouds
for each and everyone to hear…

On this glorious night of nights;
My Creator has come to live with me

and for you…

Jesus has come to

embrace you with His everlasting love,

warm you with His breath of life,

teach you the song of His Father,

Himself.

Romans 1:20

For since the creation of the world
God's invisible qualities—
his eternal power and divine nature—
have been clearly seen,
being understood from what has been made,
so that people are without excuse.

Psalm 19:1-4

The heavens declare the glory of God;
*   the skies proclaim the work of his hands.*
Day after day they pour forth speech;
*   night after night they reveal knowledge.*
They have no speech, they use no words;
*   no sound is heard from them.*
Their voice goes out into all the earth,
*   their words to the ends of the world.*

THE SHEPHERDS: Thirty-three Years Later

Were there no people in the city
who remembered the
night of His birth?
that glorious night
the star
the angels
What about the shepherds,
thirty-three years later?
Weren't they still alive?
Were they by chance in Jerusalem?
Surely there were those

from Bethlehem
who knew without a doubt
that this man was
the Messiah sent by God.

"Look, here He comes.
Such a fine young man
He's become...
golden-haired, just like
when He was born.
I thought He'd be a king,
a ruler by now,
but see how He's dressed
in clothes like ours...
a robe and sandals
and not much more.

Not kingly, not rich, but
with a certain stance
that speaks of status
and nobleness.

We saw Him when He
was just a babe
with Mary and Joseph
in a stable-cave,
warmed by the breath
of donkeys and cows.
Our sheep came with us,
we were led by a star.

A star so enormous
it filled the sky,
lit up our way
and stopped outside
of an unlikely place
for a king to be born.

We doubted not
that He was the Christ
for the angel told us,
we felt such a fright,
but he calmed us and said
the Savior had come.

His message delivered
with details of where
the Babe could be found
in a manger with hay.

Then, remember the
heavenly chorus appeared?
We were dazzled by their
presence and beauty and song,
'Glory to God in the highest',
they sang, 'and on earth
peace among all.'

We've never forgotten
that night and event.

Now here we are in Jerusalem.
By chance came we here
to be with some friends,
and look Who came also…
a coincidence?

We're saddened to see that
some care not
for this man from God.
Some lay down palms,

some yell and taunt.
We don't understand
what's going on.

We only know
we believe what we saw.
We saw the Savior
the day He was born.
The Light of the World,
The Hope of Our Lives
awaited and looked for…
He had arrived."

Luke 2:8-12

And there were shepherds
living out in the fields nearby,
keeping watch over their flocks at night.
An angel of the Lord
appeared to them,
and the glory of the Lord shone around them,
and they were terrified.
But the angel said to them,
"Do not be afraid.
I bring you good news of great joy
that will be for all the people.
Today in the town of David
a Savior has been born to you;
he is Christ the Lord.
This will be a sign to you:
You will find a baby wrapped in cloths
and lying in a manger."

Luke 2:15

When the angels had left them
and gone into heaven,
the shepherds said to one another,
"Let's go to Bethlehem
and see this thing that has happened,
which the Lord has told us about."

56

Luke 2:20

The shepherds returned,
glorifying and praising God
for all the things they had heard and seen,
which were just as they had been told.

MARY'S NIGHT

Opening my eyes for the first time,
    I blink and look around...
a straw-strewn stable, grassy hills outside,
    stars I placed in the sky above.

My Spirit's home is now a baby's body,
    designed by Me to change and grow tall.
These little hands unable to open,
    will stretch out one day and be nailed to a cross.

My feet now small, unable to stand,
  will one day walk on top of a sea.
Newborn sounds are all I can make,
  but later my words will teach and heal.

Tonight my mother cradles me in her arms,
  counting my fingers and toes.
Mary, brave Mary, has brought her Messiah
  into the world like the angel foretold.

The future written by prophets is far from her
  thoughts. Her mind is only on Me.
This moment of joy will not be taken from her.
  Another night like this never will be.

The rhythm of her heart beats close to My ear.
  Her breath warms My face.
Wistfully, she softly croons a new song,
  words about Me on this night of grace.

My tiny fingers encircle hers, pausing her singing,
  she kisses each one.
This is Mary's night made wondrous for her,
  with the Lamb of God in her arms.

A night to remember in vivid detail,
  in her mind and deep down in her soul…
a healing balm for the coming wounds
  of My mother's heartrending sorrow.

We are here in Bethlehem, known
    for unblemished lambs, far from Nazareth gossip.
Tonight Mary and I begin our journey together,
    a journey we've willingly chosen.

The lantern glows warm in the cool night air,
    our eyelids begin to get heavy.
Mary gathers her blue outer garment around her,
    including Me in her wrapping.

Joseph, her husband, always near by,
    brings the barn animals closer to warm us.
Off in the distance we still hear the voices,
    of shepherds singing God's praises.

Mary's lullaby of peace and joy and miracles,
    floats out over the sheep-covered hills…
she sings of the bright traveling star from the east,
    and the sky full of thousands of angels.

Her ballad narrates the wait for Messiah,
    and the completion of God's ancient promise.
Sing, sweet Mary, so young yourself.
    Ponder and savor each moment.

This glorious night is yours to relive
    when our journey together is over.

Matthew 1:23

"The virgin will be with child
and will give birth to a son,
and they will call him Immanuel" —
which means, "God with us."

Isaiah 9:6

For to us a child is born,
to us a son is given,
and the government will be on his shoulders.
And he will be called Wonderful Counselor,
Mighty God, Everlasting Father,
Prince of Peace."

Luke 2:16-19

So they hurried off
and found Mary and Joseph, and the baby,
who was lying in the manger.
When they had seen him,
they spread the word concerning
what had been told them about this child,
and all who heard it were amazed
at what the shepherds said to them.
But Mary treasured up all these things
and pondered them in her heart.

ABOUT THE AUTHOR

Angela Albano has been an artist and creator her whole life. After attending Massachusetts College of Art and Design, Angela devoted her life to raising her two children. Throughout those years she created paintings, ornaments, follages*, and a line of inspirational cards adorned with her Spirit-driven, free flowing style of calligraphy. Her creativity was continually born anew.

For her next creative endeavor, Angela turned to poetry. Over the last 12 years, she became a master of her craft. With at least three books of poetry in development, this volume of Christmas poems is her debut publication, an achievement bringing joy to many fans of her poetry.

Angela's creative spirit led her to focus her first book of poems on the birth of The Creator, Himself. Inspiration, she says, came to her from John 1:3 NIV: "In the beginning was the Word and the Word was with God and the Word was God. He was with God...Through Him all things were made; without Him nothing was made that has been made."

Angela's powerfully creative spirit is reminiscent of the words of priest Matthew Fox. Creativity, Fr. Fox said, is where the Divine and human meet; that when we create, that is when we are most God-like or most allowing God to manifest in us.

Angela believes when God created us in His own image, He was in fact creating us to be creators, as He is. In that light, she has spent her life expressing her image of God, and she has done so beautifully in this volume.

"Mary's Night" is a moving collection of poems that share Angela's passion for her Savior. It will surely leave you feeling blessed with an unconditional love and perspective of Jesus.

You may reach the author at angelapoet@gmail.com.

---

* In the 1970s Angela created a form of abstract watercolor painting integrated with arrangements of dancing dried leaves and flowers. She termed these pieces "follages."

12703707R00043

Made in the USA
Lexington, KY
28 December 2011